IMAGINATION

by

Mike Thaler

photographs by

Sherry Shahan

Richard C. Owen Publishers, Inc.
Katonah, New York

Meet The Author

Richard C. Owen Publishers, Inc.
PO Box 585
Katonah, New York 10536

Library of Congress Cataloging-in-Publication Data

Thaler, Mike, 1936-
        Imagination / by Mike Thaler ; photographs by Sherry Shahan.
            p. cm. – (Meet the Author)
        Summary: Mike Thaler, author of "The Teacher from the Black Lagoon" series,
        recounts his life and describes how his daily activities and creative process are interwoven.
        ISBN 1-57274-598-3
            1. Thaler, Mike, 1936—-Juvenile literature. 2. Authors, American—20th
century—Biography—Juvenile literature. 3. Children's literature—Authorship—Juvenile
literature. [1. Thaler, Mike, 1936- 2. Authors, American.] I. Shahan, Sherry, ill. II. Title.
III. Meet the Author (Katonah, N.Y.)

PS3570.H3176 Z467 2002
818'.5409—dc21
[B]   2002029257
Editorial, Art, and Production Director *Janice Boland*
Production Assistants *Donna Parsons, Elaine Kemp*
Administrative Assistance *Janet Lipareli*

Color separations by Leo P. Callahan, Inc., Binghamton, NY

Printed in the United States of America

9   8   7   6   5   4   3

To my family

People often ask me, "When you write
a children's book, do you observe children?"

My answer is, "No. I look into my imagination."

Imagination is like a muscle. We all have one
but if we don't use it, we lose it.
Everything we have, from music to mousetraps,
has come from someone's imagination.
I believe imagination is the most powerful part
of every human being.

I was born on October 8, 1936 in Los Angeles, California,
and have always loved to create things.
When I was growing up I would melt down little candles,
then use the wax to make The Three Musketeers
with toothpick swords. I loved crayons, too,
but not coloring books—I always wanted to draw my own lines.

At the age of seven I discovered the public library.
After reading every picture book in the children's room
at least twice, and *Mike Mulligan's Steam Shovel*
and *The Little Engine That Could* twenty times,
I ventured into the adult section of the library
in search of more picture books.

The only picture books I could find were *The New Yorker*
cartoon annuals. Each page laid the foundation of my desire
to be a cartoonist.

In high school I drew cartoons for the school yearbook,
sang in the chorus, and made a silver tie-pin, though I
never wore ties.
I wrote and starred in the senior play with my dog, Lady,
who stole the show.

In tenth grade I ran for class president.
"I like Mike" was my slogan.
I was swept into office by the voters
and swept out of office two years later by the principal.

I had always thought I would be a teacher until I took
one of those tests that ask—
Would you rather:
a. Ride a kangaroo?
b. Sit under a flower?
c. Write a poem?

I answered, "Write a poem,"
and the test answered,
"You are an artist."

My dad used to say, "It's good to have your head in the
sky but your feet on the ground."

I would answer, "Dad, you can't fly with your feet on the ground."

In college I majored in art. I also went to art school.
Later, I went back to college to major in English.
At that time I had a monkey, rode a motorcycle,
and drew cartoons for the school paper.
When I left school I did a cartoon strip
for a local newspaper.

Eventually, I took my cartoons to New York.
I believed I would be immediately famous
and live happily ever after. Well, that never happened,
but a lot else did.

One day while I was trying to figure out how
I was going to pay my rent, I got a phone call
from a children's book editor. She had seen a cartoon
I had done for a magazine. She asked if I had ever thought
of writing a children's book.

I said, "Yes!"

She said, "When would you like to come in?"

I said, "Tomorrow at 3:30."

She said, "Fine," and hung up.

Then I realized I had an appointment, but no book.
So I folded eight pieces of paper, made a little booklet,
and wrote a story I called *Magic Boy*.
The next day at 3:45 the editor bought it.
That evening I went home and wrote my second
children's book, *Penny Pencil*, the story of a pencil.

Penny Pencil didn't mind running his nose
along paper. It was fun because he could :
his trail. And he didn't mi? ?bbing
his top to make the trail disappear.

But one day his point broke and...

Penny Pencil

story and pictures by Mike Thaler

HARPER & ROW, PUBLISHERS

MIKE THALER
was born in California in 1936. He came to New York City in 1959 and has since sold drawings to many leading magazines. The following are some reviews of his previous books for children.

MAGIC BOY
"Children are almost sure to love this magic boy who can walk upside down or sideways, can fold in the middle, can disappear, and can make flowers grow out of his toes."—*Syndicated column on Child Behavior by Dr. Frances L. Ilg and Dr. Louise Bates Ames of the Gesell Institute for Child Development*

"Humor and imagination will appeal to small children who will identify with the boy in the story."—*Library Journal*

THE CLOWN'S SMILE
"The boomerang action of the circus clown's smile will entrance the young child . . . A unique circus mishap."—*Virginia Kirkus' Service*

Since then I have published over 150 children's books.

I have also designed games, written songs,
and sculpted.

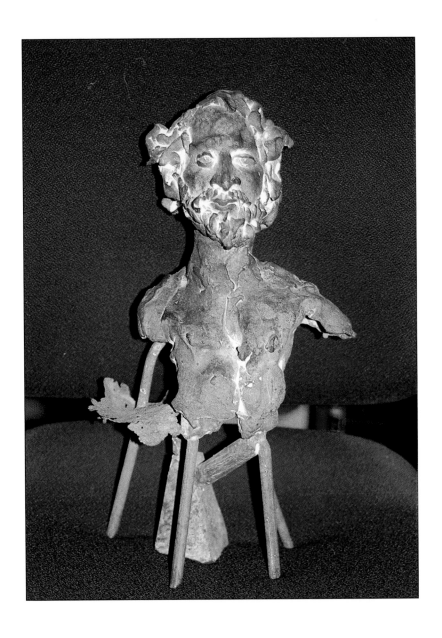

I've created so many riddles
that I was crowned
America's Riddle King.

I moved to the country where I
created the character "Letterman"
for the television show
"The Electric Company."

"Faster than a rolling O,
stronger than silent E,
able to leap capital T in a single bound
—it's a word, it's a plan,
it's Letterman!"

Though I illustrated my first five books, I soon realized that a professional illustrator could do a much better job.

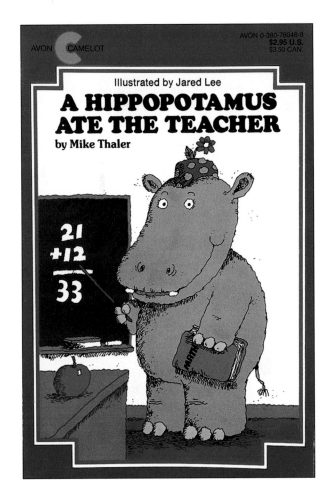

I have worked with many fine illustrators.
In 1981, I was teamed with Jared Lee for my book
A Hippopotamus Ate the Teacher. That book is still in print
along with the other 30 books we have done together.

Jared and I are a team and talk on the phone almost every day. We are also friends. He was the best man at my wedding.

Our best known series is *The Teacher from the Black Lagoon.* I had the idea for the title from a movie called *The Creature from the Black Lagoon.*

Creature rhymed with teacher and we were off!

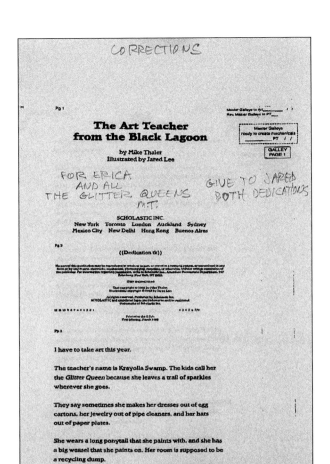

CORRECTIONS

The Art Teacher from the Black Lagoon

by Mike Thaler
Illustrated by Jared Lee

FOR ERICA
AND ALL
THE GLITTER QUEENS
M.T.

GIVE TO JARED
BOTH DEDICATIONS

SCHOLASTIC INC.
New York   Toronto   London   Auckland   Sydney
Mexico City   New Delhi   Hong Kong   Buenos Aires

Pg 2

((Dedication tk))

Pg 3

I have to take art this year.

The teacher's name is Krayolla Swamp. The kids call her the *Glitter Queen* because she leaves a trail of sparkles wherever she goes.

They say sometimes she makes her dresses out of egg cartons, her jewelry out of pipe cleaners, and her hats out of paper plates.

She wears a long ponytail that she paints with, and she has a big weasel that she paints on. Her room is supposed to be a recycling dump.

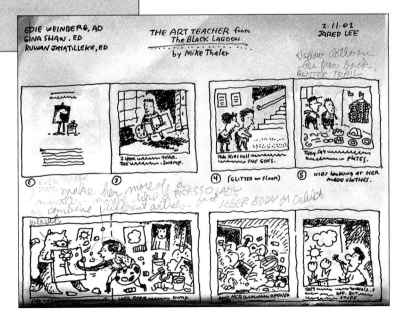

17

Kids ask me why I became a writer.

Well, I love to laugh and make others laugh.

I love to create things. And I love words.

Language is a beautiful palette with which
I can paint my imagination.
And words are magic.

You put letters together and they make words.
You put words together and they make sentences.
You put sentences together and you make a story!

KIDS ASK ME WHY
I BECAME A WRITER?
WELL, FIRSTLY - I
LOVE WORDS. OUR
LANGUAGE IS A
BEAUTIFUL PALATE
WITH WHICH I CAN
PAINT MY IMAGINATION!
SECONDLY - I LOVE TO
LAUGH AND TO MAKE
OTHERS LAUGH.
AND THIRDLY - WE
COME BACK TO
THE BEGINNING -
I LOVE TO CREATE
THINGS.

EVERY HUMAN IS AN
ARTIST. EACH KID HAS
A CLEAR CONNECTION
WITH CREATIVITY.
WALK DOWN ANY
HALL IN ANY
ELEMENTARY SCHOOL,
IN ANY PART OF
THE WORLD,
BUT THEN HUMANS
GIVE IT UP. ALL
AN ARTIST IS, IS
SOMEONE WHO HAS
KEPT THAT CONNECTION
CLEAR.

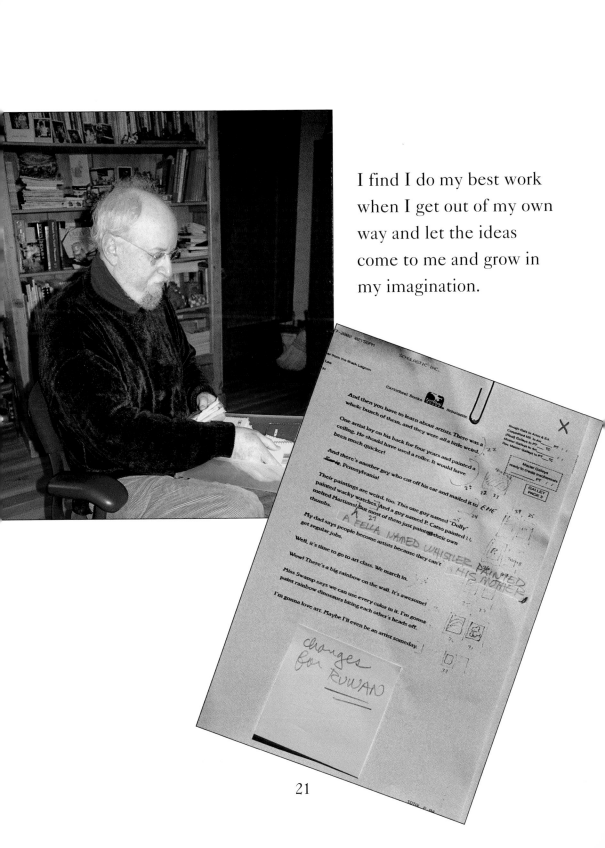

I find I do my best work
when I get out of my own
way and let the ideas
come to me and grow in
my imagination.

My tools are a pencil and paper.
Along with imagination,
they are the only things you
need to write a story.

Most of my writing I do in bed upon waking.

I had to get up for these pictures; then I went back to bed.

Until I met my wife Laurel Lee, I was a homebody
enjoying slippers, tea, and afternoon naps.
Then Laurel entered my life and led me into
many wonderful adventures.

We live on a Christmas tree farm in Canby, Oregon, with our son Matthew, his wife Tina, and our grandchildren. Two horses, three cats, many moles, two owls, not so many mice, and one chicken also live with us on our farm.

I love to be with my family and friends, eat good food,
and travel to interesting places to talk with children, teachers,
librarians, and parents about my favorite subjects—kindness,
creativity, and love.

Recently I have been writing humorous Bible stories.
Sixty of these stories have been published in a series called
Heaven and Mirth.

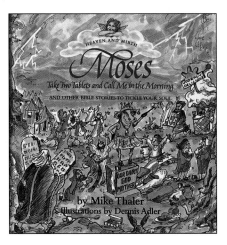

Moses Take Two Tablets and Call Me in the Morning,
David and Bubblebath-Sheba, and *Adam and the Apple Turnover*—
which includes *Lot Please Pass the Salt*—are just a few of
my stories.

I enjoy reading my stories all over the world.
I've read them to children in China, Europe, South America,
and Arabia.

I think this poem sums up how I feel about writing.

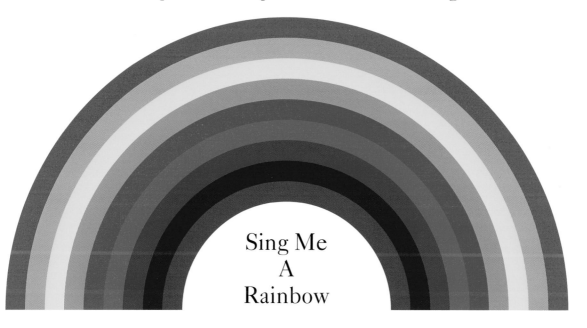

Sing Me
A
Rainbow

Sing me a rainbow
Dance me a poem
Write me a feeling
All of my own
Paint me a mountain
Write me a cloud
Read me the sky
So I see it out loud.

Your friend,

Mike Thaler

Other Books by Mike Thaler

My Cat is Going to the Dogs; Camp Rotten Time; The Music Teacher from the Black Lagoon; Owly; Make Your Beds, Bananaheads; Hanzel and Pretzel; Never Give a Fish an Umbrella; Uses for Mooses and Other Popular Pets; Tales From the Back Pew (10 book series)

About the Photographer

Sherry Shahan is a photojournalist and author. She has written several children's books. Sherry lives in California with her husband. She loves to travel, dance, and take beautiful pictures. Sherry has done the photographs for several *Meet the Author* books including Jonathan London's autobiography and Laura Numeroff's autobiography, both published by Richard C. Owen Publishers, Inc.

Photograph by Laura Numeroff

Acknowledgments

Page from *Penny Pencil* on page 10 and cover of *Penny Pencil* on page 11, story and pictures by Mike Thaler, appear courtesy of Mike Thaler. Book cover on page 13, *King Kong's Underwear* by Mike Thaler, appears courtesy of Mike Thaler. Book cover on page 14, *A Hippopotamus Ate the Teacher* by Mike Thaler, copyright ©1981, published by Avon Camelot, an imprint of HarperCollins, illustrated by Jared Lee, appears courtesy of Jared Lee. Book cover on page 16, *The Teacher from the Black Lagoon* by Mike Thaler, copyright ©1989 by Mike Thaler, illustrated by Jared Lee, used by permission of Jared Lee. Illustration on page 16 of *Mrs. Green, The Teacher from the Black Lagoon* from *The Teacher from the Black Lagoon* by Mike Thaler, copyright ©1989, illustrated by Jared Lee, used by permission of Jared Lee. Book cover on page 18 from *The Bully Brothers Making the Grade* by Mike Thaler, illustration copyright ©1995 by Jared Lee, reprinted by permission of Scholastic, Inc. Book cover on page 18, from *Happily Ever Laughter: Schmoe White and the Seven Dorfs* by Mike Thaler, illustration copyright ©1997 by Jared Lee, reprinted by permission of Scholastic, Inc. Book cover on page 30 of *Moses: Take Two Tablets and Call Me in the Morning* by Mike Thaler and Dennis Adler, copyright ©2000, courtesy of Mike Thaler.

Meet the Author titles

Verna Aardema *A Bookworm Who Hatched*
David A. Adler *My Writing Day*
George Ancona *Self Portrait*
Jim Arnosky *Whole Days Outdoor*
Frank Asch *One Man Show*
Joseph Bruchac *Seeing the Circle*
Eve Bunting *Once Upon a Time*
Lynne Cherry *Making a Difference in the World*
Lois Ehlert *Under My Nose*
Denise Fleming *Maker of Things*
Douglas Florian *See for Your Self*
Jean Fritz *Surprising Myself*
Paul Goble *Hau Kola Hello Friend*
Ruth Heller *Fine Lines*
Lee Bennett Hopkins *The Writing Bug*
James Howe *Playing With Words*
Johanna Hurwitz *A Dream Come True*
Eric A. Kimmel *Tuning Up*
Karla Kuskin *Thoughts, Pictures, and Words*
Thomas Locker *The Man Who Paints Nature*
Jonathan London *Tell Me a Story*
George Ella Lyon *A Wordful Child*
Margaret Mahy *My Mysterious World*
Rafe Martin *A Storyteller's Story*
Patricia McKissack *Can You Imagine*
Laura Numeroff *If You Give an Author a Pencil*
Jerry Pallotta *Read a Zillion Books*
Patricia Polacco *Firetalking*
Laurence Pringle *Nature! Wild and Wonderful*
Cynthia Rylant *Best Wishes*
Seymour Simon *From Paper Airplanes to Outer Space*
Mike Thaler *Imagination*
Jean Van Leeuwen *Growing Ideas*
Janet Wong *Before it Wriggles Away*
Jane Yolen *A Letter from Phoenix Farm*

For more information about the Meet the Author books
visit our website at www.RCOwen.com or call 1-800-336-5588